THE FLUID WORD

by Arthur Weil

THE FLUID WORD

Copyright © 2001 by Arthur Weil

For all inquiries or to order additional copies of this book, contact Arthur Weil, 208 Pala Avenue, Piedmont, CA 94611, aweil444@aol.com
Pricing: $5 per copy (25% discount if ordered directly through the author with no shipping costs)

Some images copyright www.arttoday.com

ISBN: 0-9676149-4-5

Printed in the U.S.A. by BookMasters, Inc.

Acknowledgments

I want to thank all the people who support my writing.

In particular, I want to thank my associate, Seth Lepore for his patience and perseverance. Seth has helped in the structure, selection, editing, arranging and layout of four of my books. Putting a book together is a tedious job, and he has been my key helper.

Seth is a talented musician, songwriter and performer. I am indebted to him and cannot thank him enough.

Dedication

These lines are dedicated to all the mentors and teachers in my life: from babyhood when I mimicked my mother's voice, to my elementary teachers and tutors in Germany, including Mr. Weinberg. An absent father complimented by and an ultra liberal Aunt Ilse fired up my mind. From high school to Army training, I learned. All is an amalgamated picture of teachers.

One of the great giant speakers, steeped in the bible and world humanity, was Rabbi Solomon Goldman, whose sermons were monumental. I listened to hundreds of his sermons. I'd walk home, mesmerized, contemplating his words for hours and days after. Frances Horwich, Head of Roosevelt's Education Department, was the founder and owner of Ding-Dong School. She displayed the knack of outstanding enthusiasm. Mr. Everett's philosophy classes broadened my mind, introducing me to Plato, Aristotle, Burke, Kent, Spinoza, Nietsche and Thomas Aquinas. I attended two courses by guest lecturer Harold Laski, the great English socialist.

At DePaul University, the drive for long, detailed term papers shaped my writing of history. Professor Reese stands out. Other teachers were poverty, fear, self-discipline and the avoidance of failure, which drove me to succeed. An array of teachers from University of California: Kenneth Stampp, John Hope Franklin, who gave a special course on the broad sweep of American Negro History. A special weekly class at Livermore High by Howard Pease, the author of over 30 teenage adventure books for boys (like the Jinx Ship), was impressive.

Every one that I worked with lent to my personal growth and learning. The misery of life and the loss of family members were also profound teachings. Thirty years of selling real estate and working with hundreds of tenants taught me much about humanity. Every trip, every experience in nature taught me something.

My greatest teacher was my brilliant wife Lillian of over 40 years. She was self-educated, a walking encyclopedia, teacher and friend.

The writings from the World's Religions are all fused by teachers. The hundreds of books and thousands of periodicals were my teachers. When I venture up to the mountaintop or stand by the ocean shore, I am inspired by the magnificence of our planet. I am thankful that I am still learning every hour, every waking day. I, like you, am really my own teacher. Ah, the teacher, the one who instructs and imparts knowledge so we can save our civilization. How lucky to be alive! Teachers, I salute you!

I thank all of my teachers a thousand times.

Photo/Art Credits

Front Cover Photo, Foliage

As You Read, p. 1, photo of Arthur Weil

Daily Living Blend, p.8, Post-impressionist painting

Bureaucrats, p. 11, Arthur in front of the White House

Loneliness, p.17, sculpture by Rodin

Life's Unique Daily Builders, p.23, San Francisco, taken from Saint Francis Hotel facing east

Acting Since Birth, p. 28, Ben Steinhorn, age 2

I Must, p.34, Donner Lake, CA

Reflection of the Moment, p.37, Lillian Weil and daughter Judy

Let Me In, p.42, Seagulls

Attitudes, p. 48, sculpture, Washington D.C.

Echo of Old Folks, p.54, name withheld

Time Will Heal, p. 59, Pinnacles National Monument, near Soledad, CA

We are so Lucky, p.63, Jeff Weil and son, Jordan, age 3

Love Transcends, p.64, Arthur and Lillian

Nature Beckons, p.75, painting by Van Gogh

One Mother, p.78, Arthur's mother, Charlotte

Premonition, p.87, Bay Bridge west to San Francisco

I Really Need a Drink, p.95, Chicago party: Left front, Herb Weil; Third from rear on left, Arthur Weil; Second and third standing on left, Francis and Jack Hoefler; Right rear standing, Henry Good; Third rear from right sitting, Jean Weil; Fourth from rear, Werner Krause

My Creation, p.97, North Lake Tahoe, CA

My Friend, p. 102, painting by Renoir

As You Read

As you read my book bits
at a time
full of tanteliz

     i

     n

     g   words

    that rhyme
        lives for
            you of love

    of frustration L

                I

                N

                E

                S

                     of praying
                     contemplation

share with me   n
                 a
                 t
                 u
                 r
                 e   at its best

let your mind wander
     your imagination do the rest

         in
         hale
         exhale
         slow – slowly

you are blessed
     let yourself be
     let yourself be free

The More I Learn

The more I learn
The more I respect humor
Life joyous, twisting and stern
Expand my horizon by nature burn
More alert, more concern
Impossible to store all knowledge
Right time – right place – imperfect
I'm not a computer

Sometimes I plead ignorance
Too complicated, overwhelmed by new events
So fast computers, new applications, radical inventions
To thrill, enthuse and pay attention
My knowledge barely scratches

The surface of great wisdom
Digested as I think and learn anew
(The right and wrong, of falsehood) or what is really true
Hypothesis, speculation all about
Awaiting change, an air of doubt

The wisest in this unsure sea adjust
Impossible to fairly judge or trust
New discoveries, new measurements, break old taboos
Our life so full of contradiction and the blatant latest news
In an abyss, in a maelstrom our mind is caught
Disseminate and must digest the confluence of thought

It's all a fairyland so real yet full of fiction
Except the history of man, the earth, repetitive or
contradiction
With latest tools we measure the deepest secrets of our life
Nourish with juices, pills and herbs so rife
Brain, computer coupled with creative vision
Befuddle on a complex scale, invalidate with true derision

Plead ignorance, just take the consequence
I ask the universe to let me live, give me another chance
Escape the quagmire of life's puzzle
Instead in many rhythms dance, while death I muzzle
And all about in six directions celebrate all senses
And ask for time, for mankind to now mend our fences
And relish as I taste, relive our history
And with new knowledge vow to shatter ignorance infested in
our mystery

Cleaning Tag

Some critics, clowns so perfect
Some so vain
With quick tongue shower mockery
They think they entertain.

In a meeting I, mostly well dressed
Forgot to remove my cleaning tag
To that I will attest
It was an oversight – so rest!

Buffoon saw this
In front of audience
Me he did so ridicule
I, the recipient ask: "Was
 this demeaning act so really cool?"
Or was the buffoon the silly fool?

It's easy to make fun of others
To mock and ridicule
Much easier than looking in one's mirror
And hear the angels wail and drool.

Race to Win

The race for what
The race to what

Money

Love

Infinity

Fame

Future

Like reaching the zenith – the game – the game

Reaching the top, momentary winner

I am wrapped up in a viscious circle
Called racing, chasing
The tragedy... it consumes me
It touches me
Its spirit is the energy within
It breeds more, yet it consumes, fatigues
Better a new start – new race

I wet my tongue for more

I rub my hands for more

I pray for more

I dream for more

My mind becomes obsessed

Possessed, addicted to more

I know I am serious

Delirious

Want to stamp out my greed

Diminish urge,
The fiendish in me purge

I almost won – but I did race and will again
　　　　　　　Like mitosis of a demented cell
Confront new demons sent from hell
A new goal, a new zeal
　　　　　　Human dream to win　　to ascend
The center of a moving cyclone, it will never end

Recharged, energized
Ferocious like a tiger chasing prey
Get on my hind legs
I focus
I shuck all baggage
A new race proceeds

Brush family and friends aside
Reconsider promises
Struggle with money
Must hurry
Must get there

Beat to it
Be the first
Suddenly a cramp in right leg
Painful, incapacitated for seconds
Just for a moment
The race begins again
Join me

For what
To what
I've been there
After Mars
How about that star

That distant star
My mind can bathe
In its light
I visualize the goal
Determined, resolute,
My collected inner urge says go... go!

Gratitude waits, thanks deferred.
It's a race, an event
I partake
A race to win or lose
Then comes another
Could not live without it
My struggle, my challenge, my hope
The cramp subsided
In the omnipotence of being
Join – let's race together!

Wish List

Most daring thoughts explode
Into life-budding illuminating pieces
Selectively I pick up these pieces
Of mental picture post cards
Wish list of dreams long evaporated
Rejuvenated in tomorrow's journey

Daily Living Blend

It's daily living
    Blend of pain and happiness
        Tears of joy and sorrow

        Towered on avalanche of happenings
Like wind -driven colorful piles of autumn leaves

    Each a secret   each an experience
    Embodied in your being, your doing
        Earned   lived
   Exceeding earthly things or money,   tarnished
wealth
        Expect the least   get the most
Touch of patience, cautious

        Most of all
  Give, receive   this daily love
          The halo is luck
Protects you from above

  Our life so short yet so eventful
     Your unclaimed eternal treasure

Paul Celan

Paul Celan (death figure)
Exquisite memoir to million
Including many of my close ancestors
Howling their damnation and ghosts in silence

When staring at your elegant
Sensuous, beautiful face

I wondered what masks
What enthralled revelations
Lips would bring memories
As tender feelings of childhood
Of struggle
Of love and hopes
Deep and lusting but not forgotten
Of children brought to smell

The roses and the sensitivity
So eloquent in mother's nature
The deliberate voice
Sexy, resonating
The awestruck audience

What power
What magic
What envy

What admiration
So much more to say
So little time to evoke sensations

Underneath the Clothing

Black dress is strong, sleek, daring

     Pursuer, lover, looker maybe caring
Red does excite
        Enflame

    Green calms with nature in its shame

  White pure as an egg and bliss

     Deserve a celebration and a kiss

Dressed in rainbow colors stills the mind

       Some who dress might as well be blind

I wonder what your puppy and kitten thinks
When you dress tip-top
         Nothing brings
   Clothing is just
    A cover up

    Then there is you

Bureaucrats

The government
The bureaucrats who sit like
Little gods
One-sided, hold aces
Do not respond and hide
Their faces

While we cry for fairness
And help
Simply ask, please listen
We the public
More faxes
While we pay your taxes

These bureaucrats
Protect their jobs
Can you blame them?

Often deviate
Are biased, one-sided
Do not understand

Become the judge and jury
Pretend to execute impartial measures
Decide their bias issue edicts at their pleasure
Make new interpretations
Callous, crude often leads to anger
Frustration and misunderstanding

When all they have to do
Is listen, listen
Try to be impartial
And decide
Solve problems
By mutual amending

The law specific
Grants me fair recognition
Instead the bureaucrats
Paper shuffle
Erroneously decide
Without remorse
Let me wait
Sentence of 15 months
Not fair
It cost me $$$thousands to appeal
Flaw in democracy unreal
Pray that you are not next!

Bureaucrats - Part II

It's time to educate the bureaucrats
We need them, must educate them
Justice is balance, open fairness
Best without an array of lawyers, judges
Festering in the courts

Surely some
Can cut the crap

Mediate, bring both sides to the table
Before advent of Cain and Abel

Adversaries often live in same
Town, same house
Help them with honest understanding

For 15 months
I have been shafted
By some bureaucrats
Shortchanged
Is it any wonder
That I border on the deranged

Surely wisdom, persuasion, mediation
Should be tied at this
Impossible station

It's OK to bring in outside help
Let the team solve the challenge
Even improve the law
Please no more arbitrary anger
Decision maker

No more, no more
In God's way settle our score
No matter what –
Can never please them all!
Courtesy ! Listen !
FEWER LAWS WOULD HELP!

Sounds in the Night

Ever late at night

hear creaking   of the house
              crackle of newspapers

something rattled

              by the wind

fans crackle vibrate rattle

uneasy
              advent of earthquake, unstable

could be wondering

         a mouse
       a rat
              a squirrel in the fireplace

Or just the wind
              why tonight

                                        scratches my mind

Eerie intrusion beneath the skin   audible

Triggers unstable, uneasy fantasies

              all I want is peace and grace

go away go away
                        get out of my face

Intimate Journey

Travel with me
Right here now
Don't ask how
Where (you know)
Escape for a day or two
No regrets
After 2 hours stop
Love and live
Wild uninhibited
Unchained
We're free and single
Alone to ask and forgive
Like hedonist, heathen
Upon impulse
Share and dare
For a moment care
From toe to ear to neck
To shoulder, lip and back
Down, down all the way
Most ecstatic, exotic play
In nature revel
Touch, tease, hold and squeeze
Experience the inner
Deep probing pleasure
Beg for more
Examine pressure point
Crevices, curves,
Teasing body parts
Utmost, no measure
Until exhausted part
Rest and start again
Like hungry begging pest
Until the flesh
Forlorn, empty, mesmerized

So muted, so well fulfilled
About to rest
Deep sleep
Heavy breathing only peep
Wonder
If the joy of loving
Longing and belonging
Will be more than a memory
Satiated, satisfied meal of moment
Once back in separate worlds
To soon the iron fence of reality
We will travel once again
Re-experience and dream
Need it be a dream?

Play to Win

If you play with yourself
You must be willing to win
Or lose
Or be handy and take the consequences
What a relief
You can always get yourself as another partner

Practical Compliment

Compliments are overwhelming
The sincere one is practical
Deserving or not
We can always rationalize
I thank you
Sometimes I even deserve it

Loneliness

The silence of loneliness within

        Painful   yet I feel good
Secure – safe – within these walls

        Still a member of the brotherhood

Still isolated   by myself,   within myself

Conscious   mentally alert

       Suspicious - contemplative – touch of sadness

I miss that other face

      I miss the audience – the concern, the care

I miss the empathy

       Outside the sea of human faces

Whose love, concern does penetrate my heart

I think – converse – with self

Unseen the glisten of the salty wet tear emitted from within

beat of the lonely heart
fate – or choice

To live as I do?   Loneliness?

I try to dissect the mystery of my isolated life.

Rich life, unexplained, magical

Habitual – little to digress

Steadfast, I admire and regret in my solitude

Devoid of sin
Searching, open-minded,
Introspective   active
Eyes closed I see the velvet pink rose petal
Symmetric, gorgeous, floating
I'm overcome with warm compassion
Outreach to touch and hug all mankind
I want to break the bonds without anger
Rejoin the multitude
So self-consumed
And share and touch exude that tender love
That binds and sometimes reciprocates
But, alas, as prisoner, this moment in time,
I am that isolate
That single searching wanderer
In my mystic world, I feel within
World's overwhelming magic

I envy the Christ-like power – the magic wand
  Erase cancer, cure for AIDS
  Blind see with new computer chips
  Strengthen the crippled, make them more mobile
  So that they can stand – walk unhindered
Wish that we can clasp hands in a human chain
  Unite the races, sexes, deviates, old, young
Still, I am a lonely wanderer facing the horizon
In a live sea of the most wonderful people

  People of all forms and shapes
Perceive the oneness with the sincere love
  Of brother – sister
Joke, laugh, help, shed tears
As natural children of a mother
  And build each day
  Discard the air of fear
  Show our humanness with occasional tear
And in the open mind see beauty in loneliness
Find that secret bowl that nurtures hope and faith and good
Learn – make the right decision
  And seal my Loneliness
  Incorporated in life's brotherhood

Much Missed

Ignorant last breath
So much missed
So many kissed
Someone upstairs insists goodbye
Some journey

Half Here

in this drowsy state

so late,   poke me   pinch me

am I still coherent   (?)

alive, eyes barely   open

I am resigned
                                    I quit

tonight   all over this world

        the trauma
                        accident, earthquake

shooting   killing   the procreation

too tired to emphasize the value

                                    I must sleep,   lie
down

others must deal   with this night

my concern   is with

                            the "mourning"

I Need a Vacation

I want a vacation, no more free time I ration
I need a rest – escape and travel is my goal
Didn't God rest on the 7th day to nourish body and the soul?

I revel, toil, my own business I stay home
A busy prisoner in his tomb

Mind frozen, little change
Confined in sameness, narrow range

Do witness my demise
Until I seize
The opportunity to change
To break the chain
Dare experiment, a bit strange
You bet – I will have my vacation
And soon! Ere it's too late.

New, modern, twisted unknown paths
Resurrect if I shall lose
            Or ignorant I simply take a bath
For I will be slightly different
In that difference lies strength
My conviction

I try the new, I turn around without restriction
The impossible – reevaluate – revolt and change
Excited I am thrown about and heard
I will, I will enter a new world!
Better go through a different door
A new language would help too

Forgiveness

Do not reproach yourself
For error or mistake
It's human
Guilt and self-punishment
Degrading
Not to cleanse the soul
Forgive yourself
Others can join but
Truly forgive yourself
In time the hurt will heal
Turn your thought on good
For good you are
Wash, dress splendidly
Make hair and face and body shine
The actor within pretends that all is good
That reflection permeates your soul
Good it is
For good you are

Regardless of age
Body contour – race – demeanor
Laugh at yourself
Humor is in the twist and angles all about
Your first new act
The deed is fast
Spells out the nature of your beast
Drastic, ease new action
Your cooking partaken in our feast
Heavens, heavens
Purgatory, hell no
Not yet anyway

Life's Unique Daily Builders

Some of us receive the golden spoon
Far too soon

Some never

    As we feed on air, water, bread
Absorb life's wisdom slow instead

      Engender ambition
      Intense our human drive
      Subconscious try to ascend
      Below the masses mingle and survive

Some of us are builders
Artists, sculptures, producers of what bodes
Creators of books, scores
Reams of notes

Other inventors
Dreamers who can master man
      Space not time

Great athletes, superlative
With training agile body
In admiring feats
Eloquent leaders, actors
Command respect from their
      Thorny seats

      The great multitude of mothers
      Each shaping, teaching, loving

Yet all these great (once babes)
Products of civilization
Special, envious, outstanding
Epitome of man's potential
Transcend thousands of species
      Of animal worlds unfurled

We are special, unique
From conscious youth
      Success and approbation seeks

Skills honed
      Swept in a stream daily
      Overtures and duties
We sacrifice and struggle to exceed the norm
As we ascend – forget that time so short – so special

If we do not reach the pinnacles
      Of Nobel or Pulitzer Prize
Irritate or follow those we idolize
Still we are the bees that
      Bring the honey, make the nest

With super-human qualities in store
      All of us possessed
Too sad, time, talent, limitations

Unrecognized great skills
Presentations
Yet through our life and offspring
No remorse

The spiral of life
Ewe travel in due course
In love and joy
Struggle in life's trips

Great feasts, outstanding
Juices we do sip

Act, reflect
Sometimes pray
That on life's rollercoaster
We can stay
Until it's time to get off

Almost Holocaust

No number burned into my arm
Just all around the inside
Of my skull
Reflected in precious gray matter
Easily retrieved

So alone
No siblings
The pavement of Hanover
The walking dreamer
No bomb, no barbed wire
No aura of defeat
Escape to America

Too late after the Holocaust
Etched into my brain

Always walking
Excited with broken English
Learned by a tutor
I was a wounded, mature 12-year-old
Unable to jump out of his skin
For you are what you are

I constantly asked
How could one percent of the population
Be such a hindrance
I, survivor, not knowing I was

Little time for love
For attention

Now later
I do retain some of my religion
Always trying to visualize the omnipotent God

Anxious to give love
I learned to laugh, to joke
I learned to kiss, to hug, embrace
Never learning how or why
With wild abandonment
Maybe of human stamina of necessity
I dug new roots

Almost

The white frisky cotton towel
Faithfully absorbs the oily skin
A new apparition
A feeling of freedom and frankness
Confined in limited, popular space
I am refreshed
Now clean
The bell announces Act II....

Late midnight
Into the brothel
Noisy, scared of syphilis

She was pretty, 5' 5", sold beads
Demure: "GI – got something for you."
I, innocent, most anxious knew
Suddenly we entered the primitive 4 walls
Door was still open, a raucous noise
The frank MPs were rustling, wrestling
A drunken GI in the hall

I afraid of arrest – lost nerve
I hightailed out – outside open space
Recouped, I waited, would she dare come back?
Waited in the moonlight, cool

Finally she came out
Gave me a glance
Skirted across the square home
It took years before
Lovemaking became an art-form I treasured
I, an opportunist, a bet
I missed – not even kissed
A lonely soldier's hormones dancing for expression

Acting Since Birth

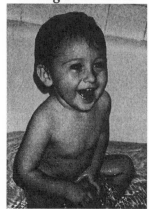

We live in a comical, crazy world.
Everything is a rehearsal
The toddler wobbly
Soft tissue, bone
Falling forward step by step
Cooing and giggly each moment
As long as no colic
Belly filled with milk and food
Oh, how cute the cherubic smile
Embodiment of hope of future

Learning our sleep pattern
Boyhood no different
Echoing a language
Of the neighborhood
Weighing the right and wrong
Uncalculated
Infatuated, dreaming of
Sonic new computer toy
Which shoes, no feeling
Animosity
Or hate, loves longing dominates
All ingrained, tamed, taught in childhood

The heart moves
Weighted, we carry these feelings
Programmed, mores cloned
Our actions target, define our life and death
Decaying like a toy
Useless on a heap
Of garbage
Bulldozed over for a lifetime
Yet some of us relish in joy
Can hardly wait to build in the new morn
Immersed wonderfully in doing, wooing and loving

Something Is Missing

I walk with double vision
Schizophrenic thought
Conjure my list of duties

My priorities
First comes work
While loving
Is foremost on my mind

Bought lottery ticket
Lost – but laughed anyway
Laughed with the rustling leaves
Languished on blanket of grass

Anguish mouthwatering
I crave some food
Lots of tea, coffee
Juice, a glass of wine

There is a wound
A hole as if a bullet

Penetrated my body
A wound in healing
Somewhere in the morning

While darker clouds
Sniff out the sun-covered countryside
Something is missing
Some kind of family

I miss that warm embrace
Relaxed in bed after my daily chase
Same tender flesh and smile
When morning light – lie there a while
I want more
Cannot have it – miss it dearly

That link between myself
Friend open, unreserved to very end
I know instant gratification I lack
The sensuous tastes I miss
Open, unplanned dear and enchanted kiss

Concern for all around

I am frazzled now
At midnight
My steaming brain
Ready to erupt
Before the volcano

I must get back
To my own preservation
Climb back in my own safe cocoon
Too late to allow adventure to sizzle
Missing that tenuous bond
Maybe tomorrow

New Smile

The mind
               a bit clouded

          the atmosphere around
   me shrouded

               antsy, despondent in   my lair

       destroy the gloom
                              action unfair

    I open doors and windows
                    up the shades

                              destroy the incarnate light
      burn out in Hades

            drink vigorously nourishment so hot
                      inner gurgling transform   my lot

      the shadows dance in soon more rosy

                         new excitement destroys
   "AS IS"

       is no more cozy
                    so do enjoy the action
        pure immense

   the gloom, dead   despondent curse

   Had laugh – giggle   ready to celebrate

   In contentment – do smile all the way home

Enamored and More

I think of you
It's true
I see your vision
To kiss you everywhere
Too fast, aggressive
Yes, but enamored
That is what I feel

Embrace, stroke, gently caress, that is real
I gently touch, so softly my lips on yours
You respond, I am fond and happy
                as the passion pours

Scared we go too far
We stop reluctantly, we cross the line
One two three more sensuous kisses
We disengage
Know that opportunities misses

Too much emotion, too strong, too beautiful
        too heady
We are afraid, cautious, let life be steady
Yet, the moment drenched
        in perfume

What are we scared of?

Only heaven knows
Let's meet again soon, very soon
Let's love, kiss and touch, swoon
The heck with earth, mirth
        to whom do we account

It's you and I that totals up
      the whole account
Our bodies meshed
We gyrate, happy, holding
Ethical, honest, longing, why not more
Two people engaged too bust
      to keep score

We know the more and more will end
Into reality of reason blend
What with the energy and time
Love fleeting, tender, joyous
      most sublime

Like a momentary picture fastened
      into space
I see, I feel, I long for more
      of movement and grace
        my face muscles into a raucous laugh
I am thankful
So alive to share with you
      this place
        Hold me, hold me close and warm in this embrace
        A bit of privacy and time – You too can enjoy!

I Must

The blow of warm and humid hot southern wind
Uncomfortably irritates my skin, my being
I go inside, the fan generates another breeze
Recline, I close my eyes
As I repose more cool and comfortable air
Relaxed and almost numbed my hulk,
And my big nose senses the air of hope, security
And for a moment I forget the world
Sense 10,000 tranquil pictures
The images of moving clouds, lush valleys
And the ice-capped mountains now reflect
In mountain lakes, while meadows bloom
My eyes now capture yours, your magic beautiful face
And I must touch you
And I must touch you

Too Much

Sad, our food left over
Could be a gourmet to the vagrant
As is the cycle of life
Procuring food and stuffing it into
      our small mouths en masse
        The focal lower center of our puss
Once down the hatch – full
Who cares – stomach, kidney do their thing
Rich arteries with oxygen now feed the heart
Sometimes too much wrong food – not smart
Except body function overtime!

It seems our search for life
Is like our search for food
New tastes, new colors
New purchases devoured, bloated
Only to be discarded later
Yes

Sometimes new friends
To be used, abused and replaced
Our adventures with lovers
Or our collection of things, whatever

There are too many leftovers
Friends – life – pieces to nourish – to share
Not forgotten! Not discarded!
Like a broken heart – pieced together
Recipe for healing
Always more, until we have too much
Stomach filled, imploded, exploded
Too much, up to here until old age
When we realize we can't fake things
      Stare truth and reality in the eye

Might as well share, tolerate
And hold on
Eat more in moderation
Red light of caution – cholesterol
Too much salt or fat
        stop once in a while
Stop – think – deter the urge
Live longer – not happier
Trite – simplistic – but sadly true

Wisdom Earned

Wisdom is the earned total
Of experience
Very opinionated – but totally meaningful

The Ultimate

The ultimate
Is the ultimate
Until the next day
When I re-evaluate
The new ultimate
Holds sway

Or is revised

Binoculars and telescopes
Through the looking glass
Focus the camera's eye
The autumn buds
The spring folly, with its 75 degrees
Jolly, happy, summer mood
No matter who I am
I always focus
From inside me
I focus on my subject
The fine strands of the hair or pupils in the eyes
Careful, the shade or glare
Development final exposure or surprise

Landscapes, ocean waves
Roaring, white cloudy spray
Tranquil hugs, smell, sound of lovers' rages
Shrinking, drying lake's decay

I focus on birthdays
Who munches cake and leaves and stays
Always back on love
That sparkle, happy look

Or festive clothes and shapes, can fill a book
Silhouettes, poses and profiles
Garments with smiles
On ball games, athlete catching ball
Torturous accident, disaster, fall

I focus on the sinew, strands of life
The helpless, aged, crippled beggar
The lines between the eyes
The neck
I love the stage
The counter
The puckered and pudgy baby face
From crying
To smiling in seconds

My camera lens
I point
Click and shoot
Scene after scene
I can't help it
I love the world
True picture
Picture of the moment
Reflection of the moment

Believe in Self

I hail you – you the reader
With open mind to cheer

Call falsehood busy
Hold your position

Molded by generation
      In this strange worldly town

Hail free thought
      Emulate the freedom of the clown

You know that truth
    Perfection just a goal

That fairness non-existent
      Only in the soul

Let the firecracker in you blast
Break out within exuberance at last

Endless opportunities
      To practice and learn
Earned wisdom reap as you do earn

Just as a fish in a sea of millions
You unique, important
        As you conjure and contemplate
        You must rebel, change openly
        Go beyond, stretch the rope
        You are the first very last hope
Your values, self-worth growing
      Ever changing still   Fight devilish nature
      Examine but retain your will

Don't let them down you
Don't let them drown you

     Discern the hollow
     From the real
Your thought, your idea, negative layers peel
       Your belief, all you,
        Be doubtful yet firm in your conviction

With youthful joy and energy
     Fight toward your goal
     Never, never ever quit!
     It's you within you
     At birth were given precious soul
     Forever ventures to be whole
     No one can steal or demolish that.
In years hence – when you see yourself from the distance
You see a bright and shining star
That made a difference –
Despite all obstacles, valor in resistance
Now in the twilight of each day
Just be yourself awake   alive   pray

With knowledge, humility
     Heal wounds
         Mend and repair
           In search of wholeness

Circumvent any obstacle
     We all must meet ourselves
       Chew on the rich bone of contentment
Keep this sight high
     Beware no easy answer
         Under the dark cloak hidden is the lie
But truth transcends – ascends – the mortar of nobility

Bloody Mess

This day, a bloody mess
Student kills four
Arab suicide bomber
    50 wounded
Airplane crashes in the storm
Children, wounded, disembodied
    In Kenya, Somalia

They say that is the norm
Somewhere in the world disastrous storm
Don't even guess
Today, somewhere a bloody mess

Stealth fighter, anti-missile
    System costing trillions
1,000 new AIDS victims each day
Blows the African continent away
Right, today gruesome helpless, confess
Hate grenade of venom some possess

Floods, earthquakes make their mark
The sky is poisoned, clouds so dark
Genetic foods, embryos are crafted
Human prototypes in laboratories
Enough, the sun just broke

Through the clouds
Still they are dying, death lurks in this small shadow of the sun
Still today is a bloody mess
And it's already noon-time sun
In truth, most of our life secure
Embrace and kisses warm and pure
In our haven mostly live in happiness
That other gruesome world, most distant I confess.

Let Me In

Give me your soft warm hand
I feel your smooth, cool, tender skin
Sends begging message: "Let me in."
Our hearts do understand
At friendship grasps – fond message, no sin
United in one vibrant clasp
So short – wish it would last

Reach out
Reach me
Adopt
Teach me
As I too guide the way
Let's leave, rekindle things we knew
Still clasping, warm and true
Without a moment of delay

So hand in hand
Our new perspective blend
Of warmth, of gently touching
Tied, for a moment, each to each other
Bound, giving, electric liking

If in meetings

Hugs and greetings
A closer bond shall shape, remain
Then sure as sun and moon and rain
We'll see each other often
And again
As warmth and fingers touch
And gently probe and rub
And hand in hand
Be everlasting our refrain

Spilling My Guts

Ranting, raving
Cussing, cursing
In an open
Sun-drenched field, spilling my
Guts and heart
To God

A cleaning, a cleansing
A pouring out of pain
Confession, excruciating expiate
Self-directed theater
So powerful, mesmerizing, engrossing
That I must be
Careful
Temper anger with reason
Frustration cursed
In control

Affair ends, event over
More ranting
More cursing
But it sure makes me
Feel better for the moment

W.W. II – Carnage

The holocaust, 6 million dead
Or better 11 million instead
In vogue, scenes of mass graves of corpses fed
Eye sockets, bundles of human kind
Impossible to comprehend by today
        most civilized mind

Atrocities, torture, self-deprivation now
        in vogue
Each people gelled in larceny, self-protection of
        its rogue
Each slept in history of hate
Invisible the enemy always at the gate
To rob our God, undermine the mores
        Sink our foundation
These evil subhuman, devil's agents
        at our back and station
Must trample, eradicate the scourge
If we are to survive
The pestilence must purge

The ancient tribes on continents in constant fear
Of drought, thunder, calamities so near
How to explain the sickness, eclipse, earthquakes
        typhoons
Someone, some people did displease the gods
        who punish us with eerie tunes

Ceres or Zeus or Woden make your offer
Take innocents and sacrifice to fill man made
        God's coffer
Be they the Muslim, Huegenots or Jesus
Eliminate the anti-Christ,
With cruel torture there

            private with clamps and screws

If their color different, their body so misshapen
Return hence you come from
            enemy of homosapien
Intolerance, only death and destruction
            is the answer
North and South Ireland feed on religious cancer
Luther, Mohammed or Malcom X
Hitler, Stalin preached but one solution

Only if you obey,
Believe, they said. Sheer obedience
Will you enter heaven in their created institution
Everyone same tune, one kind
Mind submerged, isolate in a ring of faces
No one may question, universe one mind
Their progenies to be trained in New World Order
The goal to dominate their way across the border

So if in this insane religious war
Don't count the 60-80 million dead
No more!
The institution that these master
Monster of our race created
If to survive must be debated
Stalin took the utter folly in 1943 when Hitler killed
300,000 and young men wounded forever, died
            and for what – tragedy of Stalingrad
            The new order

Cultured, advanced German
Greatest music, writers, oh so civilized
So advanced, organized
Nobel Prize winners by the score
Blind madness followed a path of hate

Eliminate the crippled, old, gypsies, Jews
     mentally deranged, deviants
With one swoop a cleaner more wholesome
     Germany arranged

He who digs a trap for others
So often falls into his own
It's easy to say sorry, made a mistake
11 million victims in death is no mistake
     eerie word like Holocaust
Many of these innocent
Defenseless children. No repentance
Can cover such human loss
I keep my mores, tradition, memories
I am one of us most of the time
Like baseball, football, basketball
     never same city, same time

Only 1 % of Germany   500,000 in 1939 were Jews
Out of 50 million – half of these Jews perished
The scythe of the angel of death
Return to avenge
A carnage of World War II – called 60-80 million dead
Systematically the gruesome, painful
Torture of the enemies and friends

Why blame the next 2 generations
     for their parents' folly?
Do we not carry the burden of our parents in this unfair
world?
Is there not enough history in our lifetime?
How much more beastly can mankind get

Yet the living do repair   in safety are pardoned
     History does not forget

As Years Flee

As years flee
Birthday candles snuffed
Business deals
Nature tackled, bluffed

I wish him stealth
Shed guilt to defy
Self-proclaim events and parties
Spend hard-earned booty

Watch his son grow quickly
As I do watch mine
Lap up each moment with joy and laugh divine

Corny

You ask
How corny can you get
In your rhymes
Better stay corny than dead

A Needed Pause

Simply go into a corner
Sit, lie, stand
Close your eyes slowly
Relax, relax
The thought consuming
Develop, envelope
Steer them to good cause
Reality, eyes open
Thankful for that
Invigorating pause

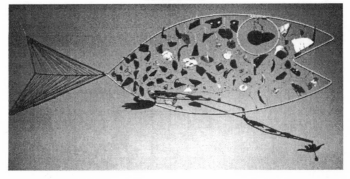

I took a chance

lived long enough

        loved,   invested

        digested

penurious

    curious

        sometimes worried
        (always hurried)

grapple   all life
    scoop in the   day

           ate up each treasured

moment

sometimes soured

     always devoured

      digested

regurgitate if molested

after a restless night

alright

only an interlude

an attitude

for juices to   exude

right   ripe   red

the body nourished   fed

to brain
to heart

to every body   part

extol

the whole

the soul

this very essence
of my being

I love you
touch you

share   with   you

you,
friends
world

what more can I ask for
while there is still time

A Magician

You are indeed a magician
Resounding, eloquent, fluid
To the finite nerve of my heartstring
Your reading, quiet yet
With deep pathos and feelings
Evokes connections, tears
As you blanket the poetic page
With a magic wand

Like a painter with easel
     Rainbow colored oils
     About to produce another
     Magic original

The power, wonder of words
Sounds, feminine waves
Wafting to my intensive
Attentive ears

With swift mesmerizing sound waves
Speed plucking on those same
Tender, worn heartstrings
Living life by osmosis
Seeing life through your eyes

Ingrained, translated into my value systems
Lives captured
Vibrating all the membranes
So titillating
Called feelings
Evoked from words, from sounds
Absorbed from the mystery
Of the air about us
Circulated by the magician

Prisoner of the Mind

Hours ago I wanted to flee

    Into the outdoors

But my conscience made me my own prisoner

    Of duty, of obligation, of habit

I've had enough
                "Let me go!"

My mental torture on a quilt of darkened deadly shadows

I must get the tools
             the cutting bar to break these

    Beastly chains break – evaporate disappear

Free myself

    the prisoner of the mind

Run away only to meet my image in some mirror

    to a better world

Away from myself

        to the other end of being.

Disillusioned Admiration

The aged burly poet
Embroidered stories
Poems like a string with beads
One beat after another

The flowing narrative
The audience enraptured
On youth, nature
Mostly on people in juxtaposition
Beginning after no connection
To sudden endings
Blinding piercing words
Mostly simple
Dried, some extra
Fluent, glue of spiritual
The bird, blue lake
Odors of food
Phrases and word – words and phrases
Just words

I listened to this great poet
Old, recognized, published many times
Afterwards I went to him
Desperate for an autograph
Oblivious he still in his dream world
Never acknowledged me
Old faces surrounding him

It was like he was slowly moving
Into oblivion
He'd made his mark

I walked eight blocks to my car
Watched gray clouds moving

The cold air chilling
I think how I too
Have a thousand stories
Evasive words
I too a dissolving entity
Walking to the gate
A splendid, sun-stroked afternoon

I would have bought his book
I wanted to – no words, no sound so
I never did
Guess I'll have to write my own

Space Bound

Some of us sketch imagination and vision
To the ultimate
After such a voyage, it is difficult
To return to reality
We are forever space bound

After

No, after it's over
It is not enough, there is a void
Sometimes we simply have to
Walk away, and feel guilty as hell

Echo of Old Folks

We old folks
Try to criticize
Lousy world
Loving jokes
Of yesterday and long ago
Dormant, alert still know
Young have no respect
Jobs were a premium, now they select
No money, no food, we starved
Now computer banks with jobs are carved

We old folks reflect
The young too smart, have too much intellect
Time our enemy
Twilight of the moment
Concern for what's in store today
A touch of love,
Simply let me go my way
Twinkles through the gray
Birth death and war
Not new – same old score

We old folks saw it before
Advertise, must have it, buy some more
New gadgets and inventions
All with the best intentions

What's mine is mine
What's yours is mine
I take it flagrantly
Lived long enough
Deserve it, authors of the divine

We old folks know
Few listen, can't resist
War engine and engine of destruction
You'll be kissed
No one immune,
The buttons pushed by those elected
Play a ghastly tune
We old folks
Believe – after all we are still alive
That justice sometimes does prevail
Old struggle between force and right
Rationalization, power, preserve with might
Edict: Worship my way anyway
Without questioning, without fail
You'll survive with most of the rest
Patriotic, you'll be blessed

We old folks hope for
Tranquility and peace
Oppose government's wheel ever ready for grease
Complicated regulations, should simplify and cease
Less burdensome taxes
And maybe healing pills for both the sexes
We old folks – though critical we do consume

With our demise multiplying hordes to fill the empty rooms
We built this country, did our share
We are the nemesis of change – so please beware.

We old folks build and yes we earned
Have some compassion, are concerned
Not easy to digest the myriad of foods
How to bend down tie our boots
Where's the nearest washroom
Can I sit down please?
What'd you say?

We old folks
Tell our old and corny jokes
How to get by
Or do we?

Not to much fried –
Watch our diet
Take medicine and pills
The washroom doesn't cure all ills

We old folks
Lucky and bitch when awake
Our constitution more give than take
Life's clock of time ticking
We are survivors – got our licking

We old folks
Have courage spunk
No choice – must survive
Somehow, some way
Despite our bitching
I guess we're still happy
To be alive
At least for now!

Coming Home

Coming home
So happy and lucky
Welcome to the abode
Waiting for me
So tired
So many newspapers and magazines
To read
The corners of each room my friends

So many phone calls to answer
So many personal letters to toy with

Fatigued
Beat
My home – my castle – my safe harbor

I'll cope tomorrow
It was just yesterday
I enjoyed the mountains
Serene snow covered mountains

My melting heart
Blending with the beauty of nature
But home is special
It is my home

Restless Within

You do not choose
    But make the bed you sleep in
    Today's routine planned
        Executed just by you

    Yet habit, what you do by rote
    Makes you the slave of your own mind

    Can you re-evaluate
    Examine inner pangs and feelings
    To better spend your time and self be true

    It is the 1st step in the bastard steps
    Not by adversity and dire need
    Power that's within you
    In the goal of happiness succeed

Share with your spouse
With friends, relatives and kids
Do get outside counsel
For you and I
For all of us are in a dead-end
    Rut
A roller coaster rut ready to get off

    We fake happiness
    We love and live excited in distress
    We complain, restless within
    Before we know it another
    Year had passed both death and birth so honored

Life is too short
    Too fast
        How long can it last?

Time Will Heal

Some cuss   some curse   seething anger
shuddering   fright   some

in   a fetal   position   head painful down
the agony   of

                                 loneliness

the perception of bad news   real   or
imagined   pain   a

dismal   sight   grown   human   beings
brothers   sisters

reduced   to   such   submission   at abyss of a
cliff

      time   will   heal   time   will
heal

Enemy of the State

I, you, we're all your enemies
At war, some hate us, some displease
I am tortured, picked on, assailed
Innocent? Not guilty! Flailed!

Why such visions of silent hate
So real, so vivid, for human rights, I now debate
To them, I am sub-human, a nether-man
To obliterate, to disappear, to destroy me is their plan

Because of my color
My race, my religion, Yet I holler
Melt, disappear
Away – do not come near
Self-righteous God your enemies and mine
Arrogant power play not much divine
Let lightning strike you in the storm
You are not part of what I call the norm
But you, sadly you exist
Booed, on the failing list
I smell your arrogant pursuit
Your pure religion's zeal so rude

I fear you monster seething in your poisonous pursuit
Knife in my back, languid, lazy, crude
You ravish good, you lie and rant
I will defy you and your cohorts to the end.
Ere society be doomed and marking mine and everybody's end

Dictators uniform your special dress
Your emblem, signatory that you possess
To you, anyone who does not belong
Live on falsehood encourage wrong

With shrill and beastly bitterness and hate
You throw stones with poison to berate
Deceiving and believing the evilness is about
Dark clouds, venomous fumes too scary shrill and loud

I, angry try to ignore you
Your numbers few, cook in your own hatred stew
Those viscious mongers with their putrid hate
You must be stopped before it is too late

We must contest and stop you at the source
Expose your ignorance, make you change your course

You have the right to talk, to hate and meet
Not to spread false witness to poison minds by deceit
Mussolini, Peron, Hitler,   stop them now
Never give in or kowtow

For goodness in each human is a precious gem
It is the sinew, sturdy from the trunk
To the stem

Honor, value and truth
Forever virtuous, honorable, heal, soothe
The racist downfall swift and bleak
Heavenly ones do measure by our deed
Thwart hate, so blind, uplift, see our moral need

For one-sided belligerent demand
The goodness lives on and ascends
The banner of my brother's keeper
Even more ingrained and deeper

The sinew of this nation's strength
Let's cherish and protect it
To any length

Infinite Borders

Borders confuse

Borders_____to be crossed

Borders   to board

Like rubberband   stretch

        Contract
                All in   its confined

        Limited, circling
                                A new outside world
Much of our borders
        are   mental

        Confined   in a   prison
        Of space

                The rat cage   The fish tank
The zoo
        The city
                The world
                The edge
                        The crossing station
I cross your border – take all – erase the border

Each side crossing the border

        Some never to return   Or

        Stretching the border

        To its non-existing limit of one unity

We Are So Lucky

Grateful look of thanks
The unicorn of overflowing banks
We are so lucky though we often do forget
We laugh and joke, censure and fret
So fulfilled go to the test
Our bodies cuddled, heavenly blessed

The dawn of challenge, ours to share
Our mission much to stimulate,
         To change and dare
We love excitement of the new
Computers, cars and movies too
Our stomachs filled
The juices within churning now not stilled
But mostly love of self and friend
Of lover now united, understand
Please understand
Someone upstairs must have it planned

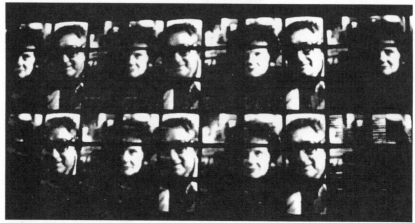

When the music plays we dance
　　　As one
We love the view of the zenith sun
Yet we seldom echo "I love you."
The daily, myriad deeds for each to each
　　　We know

We hug, embrace a million times
For over four decades we hear the music chimes
Great theater, comedy and dance
The symphonies, operas, each stance
Wars our adventure, experience
　　　Always ready to go

We are as one, rejoice in every show
Each note, violin, piano artistry
So clear, magic, music sight we see

When our thoughts spin back the reel
　　　Of yesterday

Our memories, full plate is on display
Of 45 intense, excited, trying years
Accomplishments, defying all our fears

We did so much, so fast, intense
We were the doers, builders, we made sense

Unspoken love instead
As family we shared same bed
We dared each full exciting day
Reward was inner joy, sometimes was pay

Perhaps too busy effusively
      Pronounced overpowering love
Perhaps a bit overconfident
      That automatic blessing was above

We shared our king-size bed
      With newspapers and books
We were so lucky, God gave us
     Such innocent attractive looks
As the magic couple that we were and are
We tossed the planet's magic
      Wide and far

Arthur and Lillian, quite a pair
We'd glide to the music
      Silently, applause was our flare
A touch of your cheek, steal a quick kiss
Wanting to embrace you, your closeness I miss

Our closeness, friendship, love forms did much change
Vast panorama of the vastness of life's range
First teasing, engulfing physical merge
The sexual fulfillment, nature's urge
Gradually friendship
      Entwined everlasting
United, overcoming the elements

Each victory
        Each political foray
Wonderful, exciting, hardly can
        Wait for the next day

You Lillian, great trooper
        Helping others
Your religion in deed
        A world of sisters and brothers
A deed, each act to bring
        Harmony and good
Everyone loves you, with
        Righteousness you stood
Now, I repeat and share
        My deep love and devotion
I wish you well, each day as you
        Share that magic potion
My love and hope overshadow
        Hurt and pain
May your faith in tomorrow
        Be resolute and sustain
May you realize the love we all
        Have for you

The love you share with us
        Is so pure and true
So I blow you a kiss
        A prayer of loving life
        I love you great lady
        I love you, my wife
        Departed ! Departed !

Rushing Without Care

when you're ruSHED

you're *anxious*

often careless

worry, lack

of propriety

DO IT
DO IT FAST

oh joy, when done

finished

mentally exhausted

how do we ever
get into these
crunched situations

some of us (I)
do it all the time

gray hairs and nerves

do slow it

more care next time

Line of Tolerance

where do we draw the line of tolerance

      stomach full
                   weather
(perfect)

        enough clothes   sane abode

    then comes the list :....

                              do this
                           join this
                           fix this
  have pathos empathy, you understand
                        get those
                      those this
                         protest
                     give a kiss
                       vote yes
                       vote no
                   just to show
                   donate this
               respond to that
               Please not now

    Do I really have to do business with them

      I like them,   but.....

                  Will you tolerate me?

  rub your shoe on the mat

            before you enter

Shopping Cart

Thud – thud - thud
The old man, gray whiskered, stooped
Pushes his rusty shopping basket
His world will never be recouped
Step – step – determined with effort
Slightly bent – tightly gripping the basket rail
In front of him unfurled
His belongings, his livelihood, his world
The soles of his worn shoes touch the
Hard cement sidewalk
To the wheels' creaky tune of creak – creak
Thud - thud -Thud

Though bent, disheveled,
Out of the corner of the
Old man's tired, twinkling, sharp, alert eye
    He sees all in front
The real world and the unreal
    While all about is the hot, humid air
Pressing, almost stifling
As his cart goes – thud – thud – thud

I cannot tell his age – 50 – 60 – 70 or more
His face sun beaten, weary, yet strong
That solid heavy cart in front spells
    His castle
    His belonging
    His blankets
    His plastic bags hanging over the sides
    A half eaten Mac; a pint of whisky
        Could be water or some booze left over from the night
before
        Some rags, some shaving tools, soap, a towel

Depicting the humanness
            Certain pride in a sea of poverty
The remainder of his cart if overflowing with
        lots and lots of cans and bottles
        Glass and more cans, lids, metal scraps

He pushes on his life and his life estate
        On ... on – thud – thud – thud

A sudden stop – habit
            Next to him is the City waste container – a reprieve
            Bending into the container with refuse
            Ah, more cans, more bottles – an accumulative delight
            More rags
Then on to destiny

The basket exudes smells, odors most offensive
A stinky conglomeration of odors
His olfactory glands, long used to this life's aroma

Cans of meat, soup, fish.
It is the small fish can
I can still see the white Cheshire cat
With its long whiskers and sandy eager tongue
    Licking the can clean of food.

Each of those cans and bottles
Touched by someone, opened, eaten by someone
Yes, held by a human hand – drunk, eaten
Ready for recycling.

He stoops thud – thud ... to the curb
            The spell of heat, the fatigue of the morning
            Woke from a drunken stupor
            He dreams of a cool beer
            The touch of the old lady's strong warm hand

He feels the chest pain – maybe emphysema
Too much smoking during the years
Maybe a touch of AIDS
Or kidney trouble –
The poison surfaces from time to time
          Next indigestion – not enough solids
          A cramp – another – no one cares but he
          Maybe syphilis or gonorrhea

The old man pushes on.
The world about him oblivious.
Barely a look from passersby
Just a homeless – old beggar
Too many like him –
Aren't they all the same

The cart starts moving again – thud - thud -thud
A symbol of our time
Thank You Bill Clinton, thank you President Bush
Times are very good –
For some they are good – for some...

The old man now slowly lowers himself
Sits at the curb.
He can still walk.
He is ready for his 2nd drink-a-thon of the day.
And he still lives.
Who cares! His is joyful – busy world of the moment!

Rain Drops

Year's end pure flow translucent pearl now on the run
Portions of rain cascades now by the ton
Dark, wind-driven gusty cold and gray
Hardly can discern the night from day

Is there a message to this disaster
Is our world rotating faster
Are doom and gloom awaiting our tomb
Is the earth, soft ground and flood
A warning lesson on the dot

Yet, as sure as day and night
Soon heavens azure blue and bright
The sun and warmth will hence return
Laughter spirits do rejoice and yearn

Yearn for a better world
Where hope and faith and truth is now unfurled
Where smiles and laughs are measured by their weight
Those most eager will reap reward with pleasant fate

Sometimes powerful pangs of shower
A ticklish wet sensation without power
Makes me feel wet, awake so very much now on the move
I dance with wind and pearls of water heaven's proof

The drops to rivulets to torrents turn
In their cycle our nature, pain and learn
But water is the blood for life and growth
Feeding the roots, the garden with future to propose.

Come empty clouds with nourishment of showers and of rain
In portions earth can handle and sustain
And wash into clean, fresh and most robust thought

Most vital, valued tool by nature and our mankind sought

Water, the element amongst the many elements
I, all of human life quench at your fountain and sustain
Greet you with open arms
Greet you like branches stretched to heavens once more and
again.

Judging a Book by Its Cover

The book's cover entices
What's between the pages
Tells the story
Only if the reader takes time out
Absorbs the language
Of the unspoken words

Vital Signs

The old geezer reclaims his youth
Moving sign in the window
For a block of ice

The man puts on a leather
Shoulder cover
Carries the white silvery piece of ice
Into the pantry
Below the refrigerator
Couldn't keep too much
Fresh as today
Remains short-lived

Closeness

Sometimes we seek the
    Voice of lover
Most times the body meets
    The look, the touch
    Break bread and bed
In the temporary bliss
    The sparks of the mind
    Listen and share
Close – we snack and sip the nectar, wine
Heal wounds of disagreement most benign
Absorb, enrapture in self-adulation
However confined in
    Mutual adoration
Let's hug, smile with glee
    My side or yours
      Close – embrace alive
      Hearts beat

Exult in heaven's passion play
    Contain the vibes
    The feelings stay
    Enmeshed, two of a tribe

The voice, the look, magic encounter
    The momentary trance of bliss
      The hormones dancing now in each
      True body language and with kiss

Feel the energy, the warmth
    Closeness of voice
    Magician's wand
    The hidden love
    Two merged into one

Nature Beckons

The blossom opens, pistil now so rich and ripe
Come bee or butterfly and fertilize with your tongue's swipe
A balmy, sun streaked autumn day
With duties piled, my heart held sway
Must I, should I not work and hooky play
Prance, chance, romance
      So freely foolish carefree pass the time away

I envy those who stroll so lazily about
Play or watch a game while drinking
      Guinness stout
The children jovial, teasing, pleasing
The old and aged on the bench so heavy breathing

Oh jealous of the unaccomplished
      Wasteful nothing, wit
Of romping in the park or woods
      Imitating child, the kid
Gorging down fat foods, obese
Not caring if the world looks on to please
For once to break the chain
Look up as leaves are wafting from the trees
Feel blessed by breeze, and sun and rain

Hug, full embrace with lovers joy again
Such days – often – conscious are a gem
Just like the red rose fragrance bloom at end of bending stem.
Now idolized
Now fertilized
As nerd
Instead I work
A dead anchor I do realize

In-Between Dreams

Nothing
But the buzzing of my tired ears
I close my eyes
      A dream world disappears
      Sets a smile
      A grin

Eyes open and closed
Reclined I try to venture the day
Mesmerize, cleanse
The most relaxing sleep
All the world remains

Re-evaluation

So guilty, dutiful I now reject escape
Tradition, habits imitate the ape
Late at night, exhausted
      I reflect
My life exciting, puzzled, shifted intellect

For how much savings does one need
To relish a bountiful life so open and replete
Engulfed in business weeks and years earn my pay
For time that's passed will never stay
So some of you, like me, are tied to bills and work
Self-motivated study new promotions lurk
Then from a distance re-evaluate your being
The good, the bad all aspect you'll be seeing

Let spirit, selfish dreams desire
      Become own master and ignore the jealous ire
Be self-involved your life relax and stretch the time
      It's now to change for better in your prime
      As uninvited dreams come real and faster
For those who live life balanced, love and laugh, avoid disaster

      Think success. Look from above the smile of a giraffe
And hear be lifted by the chorus glowing heaven's prayer
      So self inspired, never tired, life admired
      With ever greater want to live, most inspired

One Mother

If you are lucky to have a mother
Thank God, be deeply satisfied
Dream, nightmare, scare I barely wake
Alive, dead, alive my Mutti now for heaven's sake

Long dormant gray cells make hives reappear
She comforts still, she holds me very, very dear
Don't worry, she approves or disapproves
Believes with overflowing love and deep affection
Protects me from all the fright and fear
I am special – that unique human child
Her kid, her offspring
Her flesh and blood, ever tied
To some mystical imaginary umbilical cord
I love you son her soothing whisper
Will help you son sincere her hope
Can do no wrong
Her burdensome song

Her gentle face so vivid and so near
Enthused, protective, responsive and so dear

Her tone and mine are shockingly so real
"Here, have some soup," her calm appeal
I feel so joyous, yet so deeply dread
I now awake, it's early morn
In shock for mother
Has long been dead

Yet love, fondness, vision, dreams are real
The memory like yesterday no human can deny or steal
I want to hold that image, can't for long
The childhood tunes transformed in serious adult song
There's duty living, work-intruding world
I pressingly do understand, reshape her now unfurled

Secretly to heaven, my outstretched arms point mother
My open hands I see her face, her eyes in space
For the dream and mystery are heaven's send
And she is – will always be with me –
My mother blessed, my dearest closest, loving friend.

100 Pages

I could write 100 pages of platitudes
Which add up
To 100 pages of platitudes

Unless the reader sits, stands up
Takes an interpersonal rest
Finds new venue
New perspective

My platitudes will be blown to the
Wind of more platitudes

Time to Celebrate

sun shines
heart beats

TIME TO CELEBRATE

baby cries

daffodils are in bloom

fish jump for insects

they say *I do*

tantalizing meal is served

This is a special, special day for us

lazily lying on the sandy tropical beach

climbing expansion

Spectacular view from the upper ridge

embracing tenderly
touching your lover

driving your new car for the first time
moving into your first or second house

Seeing the child's robust smile   innocent joyful
laughter

hearing the words   I love you

Understand   understood
breathing the words
it's not cancer

80

RUMINATE *(Almost a Death Wish)*

Now at dawn, luck
Like young free fawn
I live
Have only 5-8 more years
Don't look sad
No salty tears
Three quarters of a century
I followed my nose
My education I chose
My partner, my house
Events

Rooted for 40 years
On the same block
My foolish choices
Too late I mock
What to do in the next five years

My body shows
Too many duties still
Prisoner of my own soul
Even tomorrow is accounted for
I feel like crying
So wanting to avoid dying

A slow and stagnant future
With little hope
Much, much to see & do
It is so much harder
For aged to move
To build and produce

In the twilight of my years
I'm wise, I choose

Who in the world will listen
Even of my gem, go glisten

I was on life's boat
Got off
Now miss it
I turn eager daily
In circles about me
A busy dutiful word
Unfurled

Each next bite
Sleep late, up in the dark at night
Still tomorrow
Surely is mine, must reshape my habits
Master the wrong design
I must have done something right
Somewhere – sometime now

Enough poppycock, grabble, rattle and raving
Predictable and behaving
Must break that bond
I will not be forgotten
And if I am – I won't know the difference!

Control by Magnetic Waves

The compass needle
Mysteriously points
Uncovered force directed
From the earth's mass

I, the earthling
Ghost cavorting with my nature
Follow an unexplained course
Directing all my thoughts
Values
What controls my body
My actions to do, to search, to love
To survive
What controls your body
Is it magic

With all the drumroll's noise
What do I choose
Why at this moment do you read
Why urge, curious and needy
To win
Does not mean success
I do sustain
The waves bombard my brain
Are they so lame and tame
Create that surge
That urge
Beyond control?

Infatuation!

It seems, it has been a long   long time
                    So good to see you
Come close!
                    Let us embrace and hold

First feel and grasp each other's warm exploring hands
                    And as our fingers touch

Next gentle kiss on cheek, on neck, on lips
                    So moist, electric, sexy

For a moment we are lost in space, in time
                    Re-awakened rapture

Stay close – as upper body parts do press and touch
                    It feels so strong, like thunder

They say it's chemistry   I fully, heartily agree

I do restrain my hands – so tempting – apt to wander
                    "I miss you" in quiet whisper, I reveal

I miss you very much! I long for you!
                    How wonderful this special feeling.

You say you must already leave. Obligations?
                    Stay, stay just a while, you know you miss me

"Have you forgotten? It was but yesterday we parted!"
                    It's been a long, long time.

84

Manmade Rules

Release the ten commandments
Shed all materialism
Re-evaluate your modern religion
Something new to build on

    Self-respect
    Self-adulation
    Self-preservation

In a great sea of predators
The tiger shark anxious
Called human
Still does awe nature and the God
The power of the realm
With man and God as its conception

Imagine of understandable
Different
Illusion religion
Awe for the deity
Simple for the simpleton
But meaningful profound for
Most sophisticated

Yet power of belief
Regardless of its roots
So strong – to cause
To cause most bestial denial of all contrary
And armies go to war
Conversion in the name of blood
Sheer subversion to the cult
Man-made the rules and dictums
All blind followers of supposed heroes
Yet were victims – servants of those rules

Until some rational counter force
We are humans
Each to choose our course and God's
To modify belief to serve mankind
Not destroy it

Somehow we do believe –
Each have our God – our deity
Be it an angel or the devil
It festers in our superstitions
Ingrained in codes and mores in our daily life

The mystic power – without thought
Or worship – contemplation
Would be meaningless
The holidays, the codes, the customs
It's inside your/my head – your/my body
Imbalances the balance of your daily action

All bound by a force of laws
Fair and futile in loose unstable soil
Few laws are fair to all
Free and complex our society
I howl at the world

The problem:
The world howls back
With gusto and venom
And Gods thunder and laugh
Dare ask the question !

Premonition

He had that premonition
That this was it
The rich, ripe, bundle of green grapes
From Chile, tempting
Begging to be eaten
Better not

Hurry on to work
Sell a few more houses
Cold calls
The huge stationery discount store
Offered a new fax machine

I'll keep the primitive old one
Why waste the money
He knew he could afford it
Old habits hard to change

That evening at the public dance
Live five-piece band played oldies
Graceful slim
Voluptuous ladies eye him
Waiting to be asked
He did

He damned danced galore
Little conversation must damn

He spied a pretty brunette fair
High heeled, communion
His world of theater and classics
Was foreign to her
There was some chemistry
Still two sets of dames were enough

Ample choice
May dance
In simple tasted dresses
Slacks

Maybe he too
Had lost that sense
Of attraction, dark blue wool pants
Suspenders covered by a leather vest

But it didn't help
The silver white hair
Face wrinkles
The rotund stomach gave away

Despite the brisk quick step
There was loneliness in him
He drove home alone
Thankful for the exercise
She died, after 40 years sharing
Bed sheets
She died four years ago
Pieces of the heart
Each, a bleeding memory
He simply couldn't go out
But did

Returning to his shell

Each month, each year
Time passed Him by.
He liked the sweet green grapes
Seldom ate them

He missed that warm body to touch
Felt each night the pillow without face
He knew time passed him by
Grand recommendation
Entertainment ate up the evening hours
Time passed him by

The greatest fright
To wake up the next morning
Who will find me
What legacy will I leave
His life so empty selfish
Full of things with little substance

He went to several funerals
More each year
When would his time come?

There were dreams
Dreams of love, old close encounter
Of meshing, messaging, teasing
Dreams – entwined, luscious lips,
Enticing, spirited, wonderful
Some of them real – not dreams

Days merged quickly into months
And years

He moved slower

Forgetful
Always busy
Busy with himself

It hurt
He knew it
That there would be a tomorrow
He was full of it
As his heart still broke daily
Into a thousand always self-healing pieces

Cashmere Sweater

Double (2)

Soft Sweater

Knit

Cashmere   sweater

As winter comes
Such comfort bestowed

The long,   soft
Knit

Miraculous comfort

Distinctive design   blues   yellow   light

Out of cramped closet

Into the drawer

Little moths neatly cut   swath

So holy   now(hole-y)

        Despite a few holes   so soft   so gentle   sexy   smooth

Two-ply   design unique special

Cashmere wool a special God given blend

                        Who cares about a few tiny moth-eaten
protrusions?

Breezy cold outside – it makes my day   inside and out

Always the magic softness – lightness – warmth

The sweater and the man inseparable   holes yes

                                I wear it anyway
    Console some souls

Yes, last year's sweater

                                Was somewhat
better

This one unique   There is nothing like it !

            A heaven's gift   a heaven's touch

                Please   no comment

How Could She?

Fourteen years my housekeeper
Washed, cleaned
Vacuumed, did dishes
Knew every wrinkle, corner
Once a week
I gave her my full trust

Six months ago
I bought $500 traveler's check
Went on vacation
Misplaced it
Then she found them
Only $400
I thought I had $500

Being absent minded
Maybe I spent the $100
Thank you for finding them

A month passed
An express audit
You received $500
With copy of $100 check
She forged my name and cashed it!

On the check
The signature was mine
But some letters were not mine
I have done 25 years of notary work
Became an expert on signature
They don't change in decades

When a person of sound mind
Steals from a friend

From her employer who trusted her
Crazy. 15 year employee
The check for $100
Was made out to her
Lousy forgery of my name

I have few friends
Trust them all
Few confidant

I trusted this person
Implicitly with my house
My burglar alarm
Drawers, money had been missing
Over the years
Now I know
I am devastated
Now I know why
Some of Lillian's jewelry was missing
When she died four years ago

This trusted housekeeper had $20,000
In my will if I die for her!
My stomach is in knots
Tomorrow
I will change
My will
I feel so sad, so downtrodden
So disappointed
One of mine, like my family
I cannot even shed tears

It's like a friend died
So did my trust
Belief in myself
Help me restore my trust.

Lucid Early Morning

Why am I most lucid
    Inspired at 3 a.m.
When the world sleeps
The moon scampers around
At the other side of the globe
    Revel in daytime
The motor from some jet drones overhead
I wonder how I can program
    My inspiration better
The newspaper delivered
The TV anchorman waking up
Somewhere a baby born
The raccoon at work
The cat busy at play
I stretch the day
    How can you stretch time?
Researching, produce, plan 15-18 hours
    Into the early morning silence
Some of us are isolates
Harmless deviants, doing
Our thing
Mind open, active, challenging
Never bored!
It's 3:15 a.m.
    I better go to sleep
I'll hate myself in the morning
Dead tired when I awake

I Really Need A Drink

I really need a drink

                           albeit a glass of wine

           shot of whiskey

I'll settle for a cognac

                        After that my innards

           will inflame the world

I will proclaim my innocence

                     by word, by deed

troubadour
           pronounced adoration
of your beauty

                   overflowing with love

prized compliments

                            the damn lies

of love ever

              invented

the second drink

              of course

          Slight blur   less pain

most helpful

              The languid lingers on my lips

Must have another

A Look at the Past

History does not repeat
Great enemies are dead
The ruins trumpet sound of yesterday
The super race demise
No civilizations come and go
So where do we fit in?

My Creation

I created a chain of words
Into rhymes   Into poems
My words
You, anyone educated
Could have written

I did it
With the help from my spirit and heaven
Some psychic, crazy brainwave
It is my creation
My book
That I love to share with you
It is my struggle between things
And thought

If I sound like a raving egotist
At this moment I AM ONE
Self-fulfilling, grandiose
Now I crave free flow
Sometimes words magically cling

Between materialism
The beauty of nature

Between comfort or the unknown
Spirit
Irritating the human mind

Sure, I need food, sleep and clothing
Still I, with human intellect
Need my share of the spiritual
Pleasure, feed, play with
And reap reward from our 5 senses
The feelings
The arts, of music
Appreciation of the earth beneath our feet
Born yesterday, born today
Reborn tomorrow
That is the beauty of the newness of life
Inject ourselves with a new dose
Of energy
Of positivism
Of love
Of faith
Of hope
My creation

Simple Utopia

The arrogance of yesterday
Deep criticism will soon burn away
A more gentle, civilized arrival
Shower compliments
To all that we are
Vital and alive

The Bell

Of doing
Somewhere the bell announces
The minute
The hour
The year
My life
My finality
How much time?
Demise – all power is benign
The ticking clock supersedes all wealth
Remnant my vitality, creative brain and health
Eclipse of the moon so phased
No time to wait or waste
Just one more time exposure
A flash – the last composure
Too late the bell has rung
Better pose my best...

Who Else?

Self-anointed
Self-appointed
Self-aggressed
Goes a long way

Who else but you
Can change rainbows
Excite, enliven every day

Young at Heart

An old man   young at heart

    I'm home

        Alone... anxious

              untamed

   all hours

        sleep when needed

nothing heeded

        invigorated – stimulated

        the company of electronics
          few visitors

    up until 3 a.m.
                relentless

   new thoughts   old memories

  starting projects

         conjuring, poking around

Creative in a bath of freedom
            never finishing
    roaming

      forestalling the inevitable

But One Love

I have but one love
So intense, so powerful, so tough
For you, yes   just for you
So deep, so very much sincere, so true

I love your smile
Your piercing look, your style
So much! I love your tender touch
Each deep pronounced and piercing word

Each sharing wish of hope and hurt
You are my entrée and dessert.
I love the messages we do exchange
The magic love of human range

As I pronounce my love to you
Without inhibition, so powerful, so rich and true
So you extend your love to me
Mysterious bonds I do want to exchange with joy and glee

Flirting, teasing, pleasing, foreplay
Consumed our meeting yesterday
We are way beyond the touch of lips
My transformed healing potion you must sip
Fast pace of past we shared each day
Engulfed in work, in charity and play

In love of God and world and deep respect
Despite emotions, playfulness we'd not elect
Our daily prayers are for inner peace
Devoured books, anecdotes and pleasantries
Share gourmet feasts
Prepared with zest, artistic for us
So thankful to partake in such riches of love

My Friend

This sense of freedom

      Unknown tomorrow

            A magnet (inside) me

Like radio waves   so

   sca   tter   ed

Can I ignore you

        I am my own enemy

Won't tell you tomorrow's surprise
I'll smell, taste anew with open eyes

    Embrace with grace

Surprise where I am

Where are you
Where on earth

Is our place

Our spirit out of body

Floating
Right behind you

FREE IT

It is your friend

and you know it

False Friend

If it hurts, it's hideous
If a friend ruins my good name
Belies my true intent
Behind my back, tells most untruth
In circle claim reverts its contempt
It pains me, for I've lost you friend
False friend better off without

Good riddance
He'll trip on his venomous mouth
Few will miss him

Who Measures Success

Success is measured

by the beholder

envious world

critical and bolder

compliments of out   standing

deeds and feats

public approval

on a pedestal with honor

monetary reward

success comes to many shapes and forms

It touches the heart

It increases the bank account

soon dissatisfied on roads

to new success

success the blood and guts   always competition

the honor, purse and approbation

104

          success elevated to   a new station

Stand like a giant   You have made it Life fluid like a
river

        You, the parent   the friend   the helper caregiver

Each plateau of success   yours to decide

Careful: Don't let it go to your head – and swell

            You've made it

      Success is the self-satisfaction   within

You've made it   in humility accept

         Whether earned or luck

      We the doers succeed on many levels

You made it today   Yes you did !

       Not everyone can say that often !

They are waiting for you   want to knock you off as king of
the hill

How lucky that we can be thankful!

April Fool

Keep your cool
It's April fools
Spring has sprung
The lark has sung
You simply hold your tongue

April fool
Sit on the stool
Watch one leg uneven
Slipped, whacked behind, you are believers

April fool the year that ended has
     Just started
Ice cold, frozen drift has parted
The hope of spring
Reborn, rejuvenated, new does optimism bring
The music, melodious sound I sing

April fool with hope and sun
Bring hopeful new predictions frolic fun
Yet share with job, with duty and with work
Yet time for courting, loving vibrant is our perk.

Crumpled Paper

She dropped the crumpled paper
He stopped to recover
As if it was a handkerchief
Of old times

Was it a divorce decree
A love letter
A disgusting warning

If she did not accede
To his wishes

He'd expose her

Tell the world of the trials
Their secret affairs
Her admirers
The yellow press
Would revel
In the racy juicy journalism

It was none of them
The crumpled paper
A rejection, an actress
Over the hill
Superseded

She rated number ten
Not number one

He unfolded the crumpled paper
Breathed in her face
Next to him

Dearest, I Love You

Dearest,
I love you
When can we meet again

She shifted, elated
Let's leave this damn party
And celebrate

They did

Every Time I Eat

Every time I eat
I nourish
My soul

Magic arteries
Carry the transformed
Food

To brain
And Heart

Enthuse the engine
Of
The body

Recharge grey cells
To make
Decisions

For my destiny
And yours

Our Work Routine

Time, Age wear on us

The maturity, lessons earned

Lessons learned

Years slip by - convinced

We never age! We never die!

Look in the mirror of your childhood

Look now

What will you look like ten years hence?

I mean from head to toe

That is you

Your voice similar

Your intonation the same

Hear me

Do more! See more!

Worry less

Time out for enjoyment – R & R

The work will be there soon enough on Monday

Garbage In and Out

Garbage in and out
So is our life
Confluence of ideas
Nurtured, digested, tested in and out
A lifetime of shaping
Tight pressures, acceptance, regurgitation
Open, not insulated measures
Our monthly intake enormous
The garbage of the mind
Explosive, ample, blind

Away, push out, store elsewhere
Cleanse the thought-avenues of day and life
Wrappers, packages, bags
Which carry food into our small mouths
Amazing garbage
What we say and forget
Pontificating in arrogance
Torrents of words, always a chance
Questions, directions, commands
Acknowledgements, more garbage

Only when I finally find
Total stillness - total silence
At peace within myself
Listening to the beautiful spirit
Of space, the universe, the realm
Complete with pangs and pain
Charting a clean new course
Through the heap
All around
Do I see
Nature's recycling includes me

A Fresh New Book

A fresh new book

Unread

Wasting prestigious on the shelf
Words sealed, unrevealed

Until suddenly

Adventurous new reader
Dares to read

Devour, tower
Comes so alive
Black ink into vision pictures
Stories
Emotions

Each a new adventure

The End
Back on the shelf

Wait a new millennium

Why are so many of us books
Almost dying on your shelf?

Other Titles by Arthur Weil:

Life, Love and Gems That Shine	$8.00
Exploding Mind or (Not Over the Hill Yet)	$5.00
Poetry is for Sissies	$5.00
Reflections of the Moment	$5.00

All books ordered directly will have a 25% discount with no shipping costs. Contacts can be made by e-mailing aweil444@aol.com. or calling (510) 654-5626.

Books can also be ordered through amazon.com.

These books make excellent gifts and are autographed by the author.